STRING BASS

I0798698

Elementary Scales and Bowings

for STRINGS

by HARVEY S. WHISTLER and HERMAN A. HUMMEL

CONTENTS

RUBANK®

HAL•LEONARD® CORPORATION

7777 W. Bluemound Rd. P.O. Box 13819 Milwaukee, WI 53213

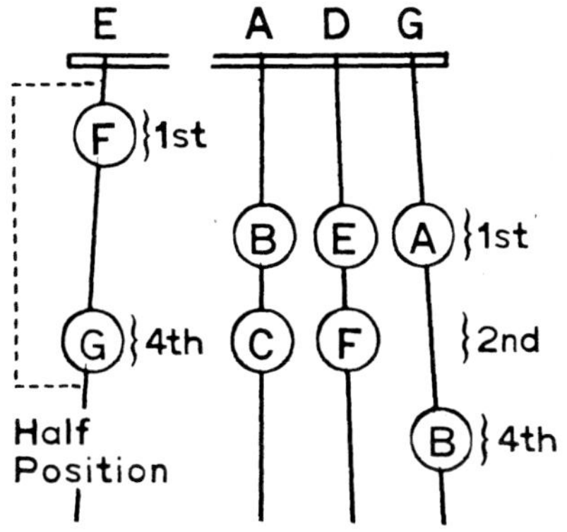

Key of C Major

Détaché Scale

Use whole bow with détaché bowing.

Slurred Scales

Legato (Smooth and connected)

Detached Bowings

Broad and detached

Staccato (Short and detached)

Bow Division

Détaché Scale in Quarter Notes

9 

Use whole bow with détaché bowing.

Broken Chords

10 

11 

Tone Study

12 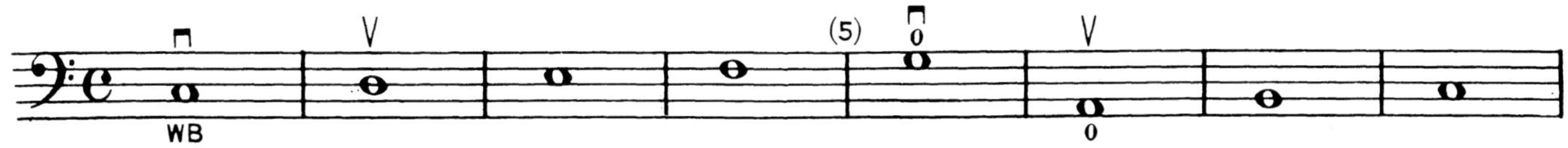

Also practice very slowly, sustaining each tone for EIGHT counts.

Eighth Notes

13 

Also practice (1) slurring each TWO notes, and (2) slurring each FOUR notes.

Quarter and Eighth Notes

14 

15 

16 

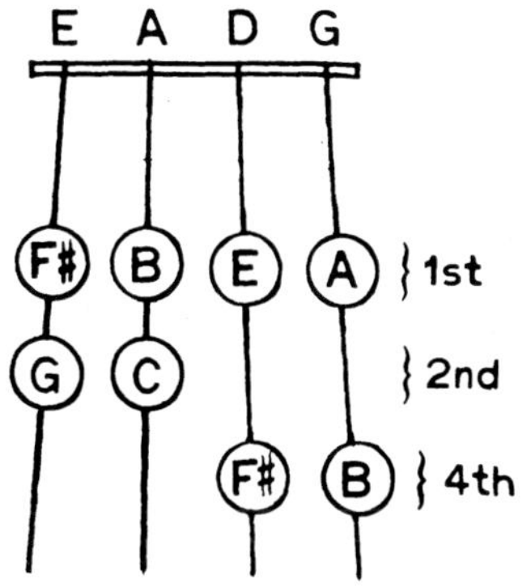

Key of G Major

Détaché Scale

17 

Use whole bow with détaché bowing.

Slurred Scales

Legato (Smooth and connected)

18 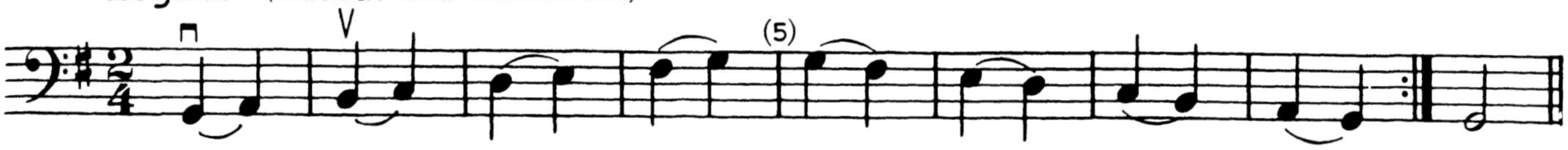

19 

20 

Detached Bowings

Broad and detached

21 

Staccato (Short and detached)

22 

Bow Division

23 

24 

Détaché Scale in Quarter Notes

25 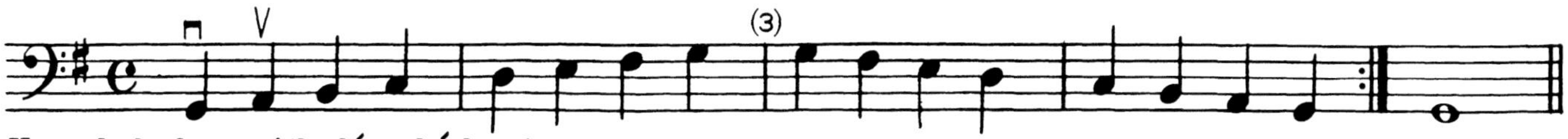

Use whole bow with détaché bowing.

Broken Chords

26 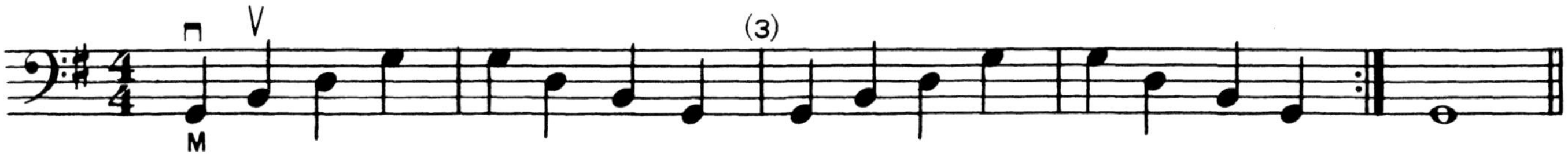

27 

Tone Study

28 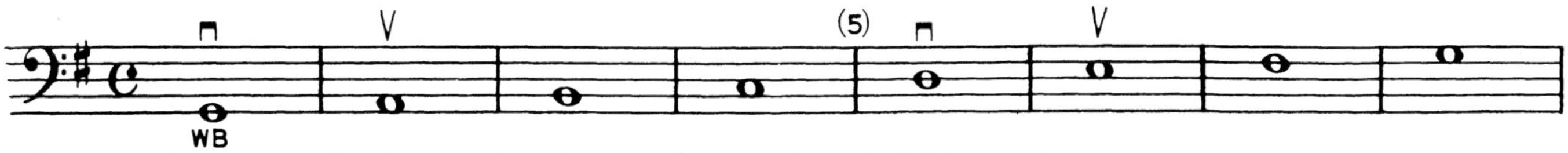

Also practice very slowly, sustaining each tone for EIGHT counts.

Eighth Notes

29 

Also practice (1) slurring each TWO notes, and (2) slurring each FOUR notes.

Quarter and Eighth Notes

30 

31 

32 

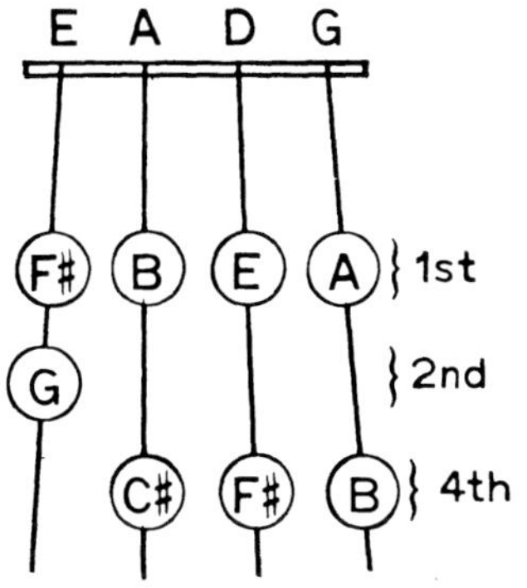

Key of D Major

Détaché Scale

33 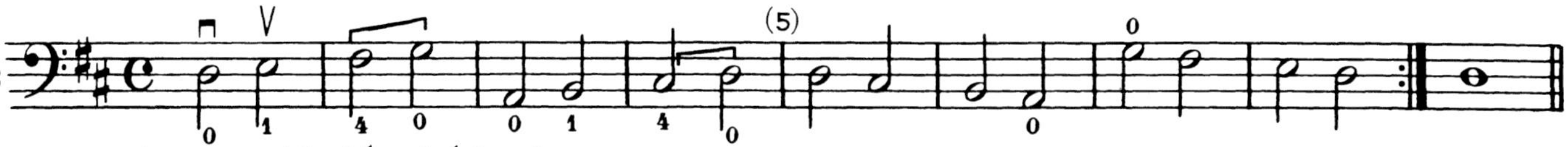

Use whole bow with détaché bowing.

Slurred Scales

Legato (Smooth and connected)

34 

35 

36 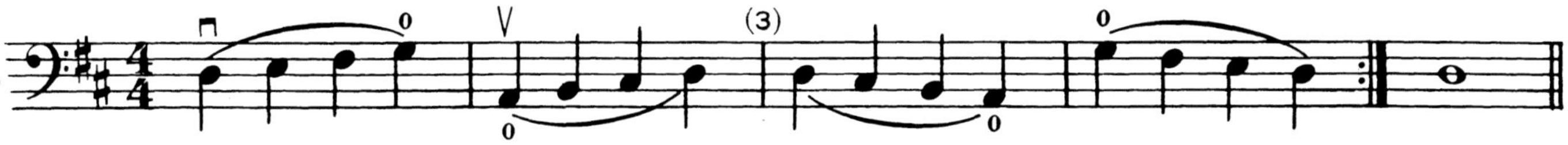

Detached Bowings

Broad and detached

37 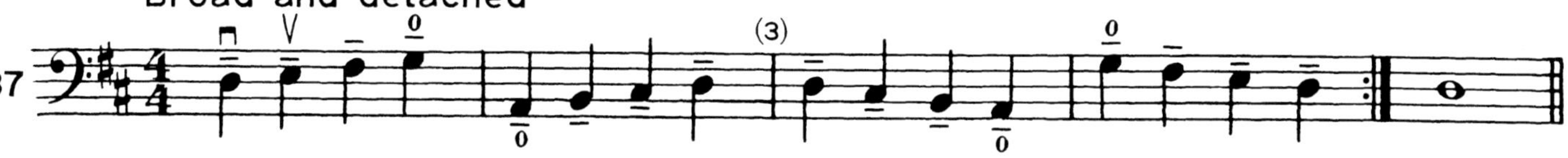

Staccato (Short and detached)

38 

Bow Division

39 

40 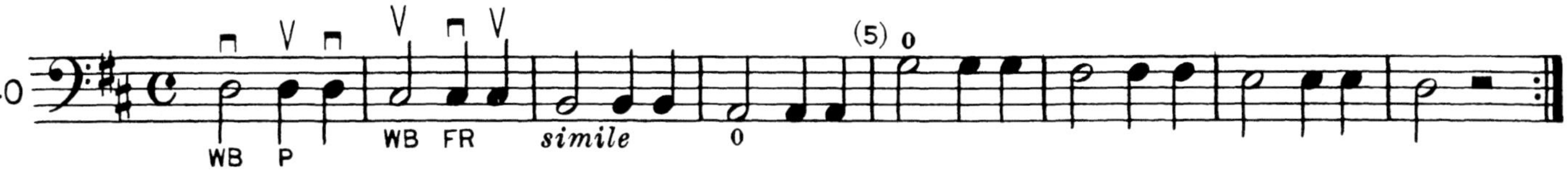

Détaché Scale in Quarter Notes

41

Use whole bow with détaché bowing.

Broken Chords

42

43
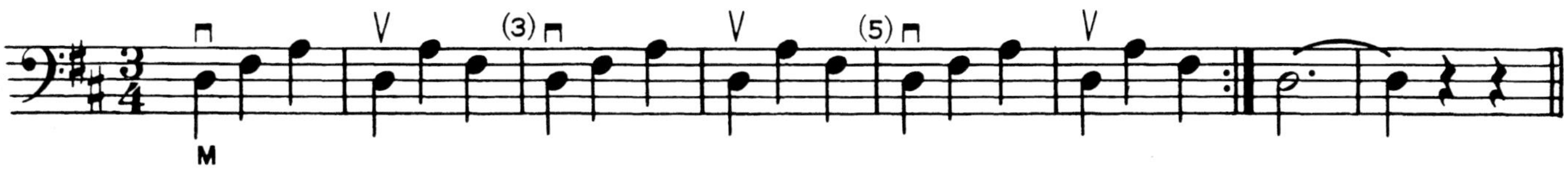

Tone Study

44
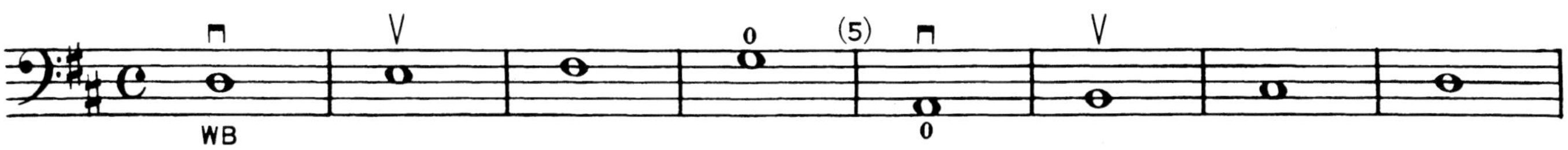

Also practice very slowly sustaining each tone for EIGHT counts.

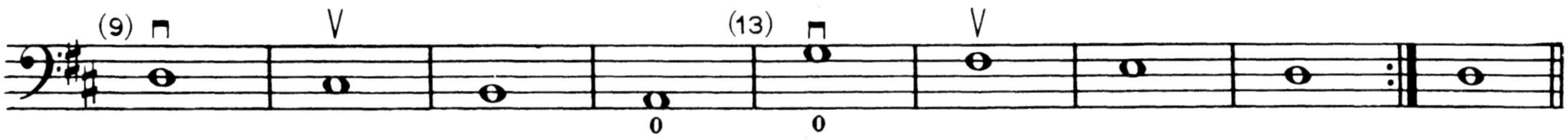

Eighth Notes

45

Also practice (1) slurring each TWO notes, and (2) slurring each FOUR notes.

Quarter and Eighth Notes

46
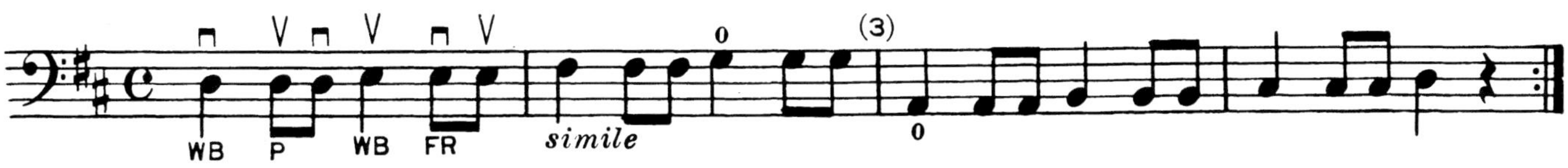

47
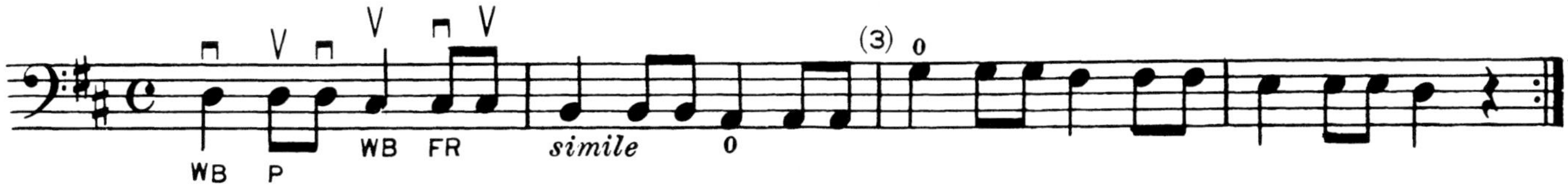

48

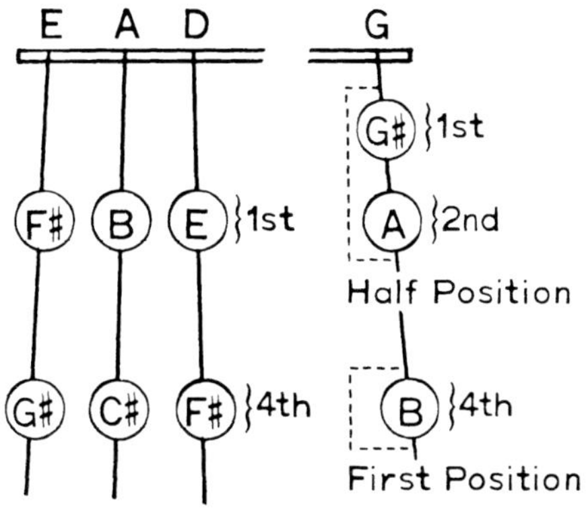

Key of A Major

Détaché Scale

49 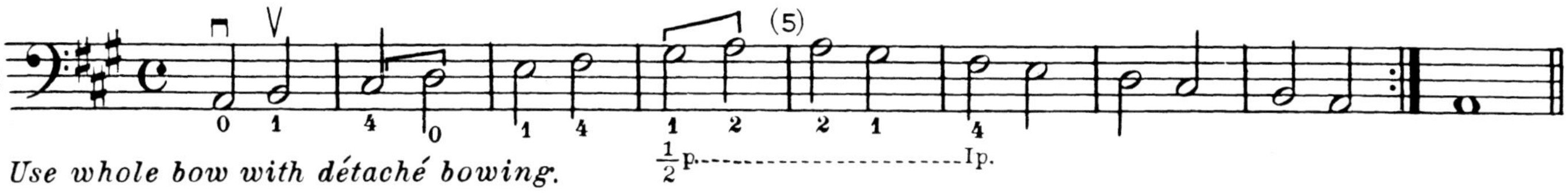

Use whole bow with détaché bowing.

Slurred Scales

Legato (Smooth and connected)

50 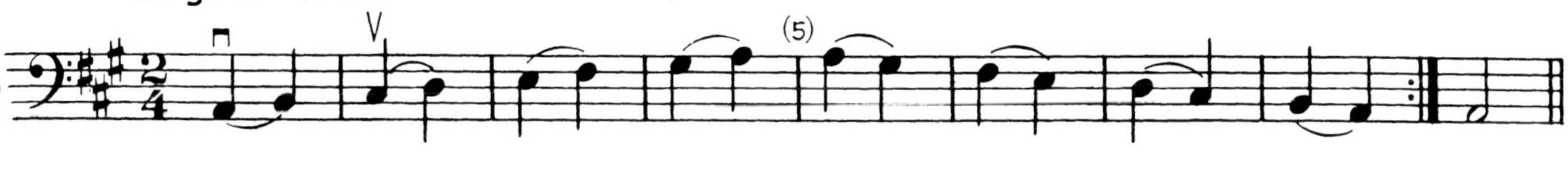

51 

52 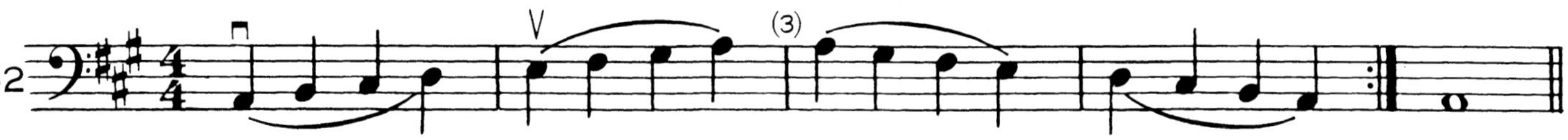

Detached Bowings

Broad and detached

53 

Staccato (Short and detached)

54 

Bow Division

55 

56 

Détaché Scale in Quarter Notes

57 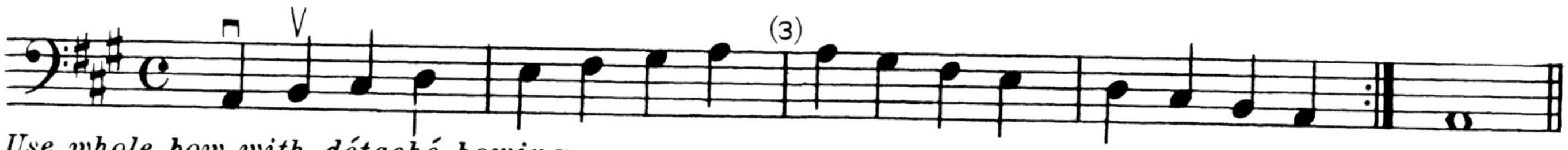

Use whole bow with détaché bowing.

Broken Chords

58 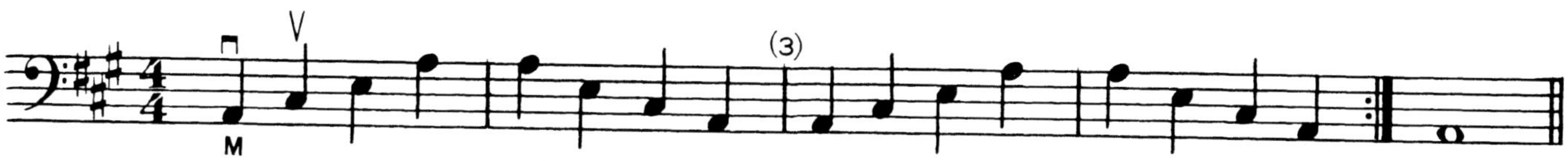

59 

Tone Study

60 

Also practice very slowly, sustaining each tone for EIGHT counts.

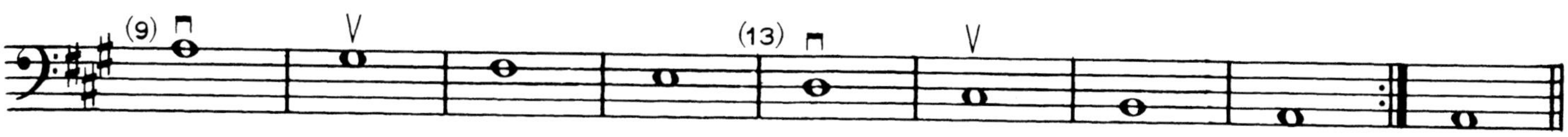

Eighth Notes

61 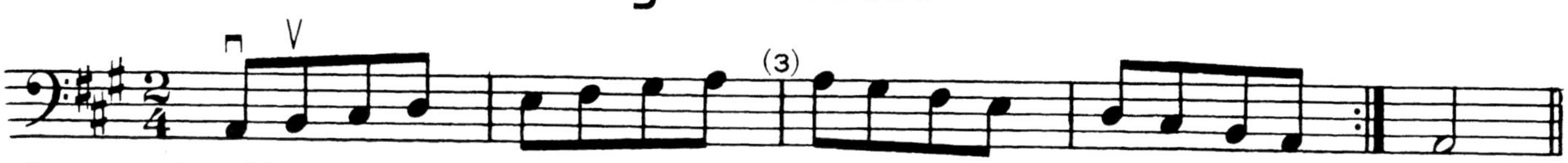

Also practice (1) slurring each TWO notes, and (2) slurring each FOUR notes.

Quarter and Eighth Notes

62 

63 

64 

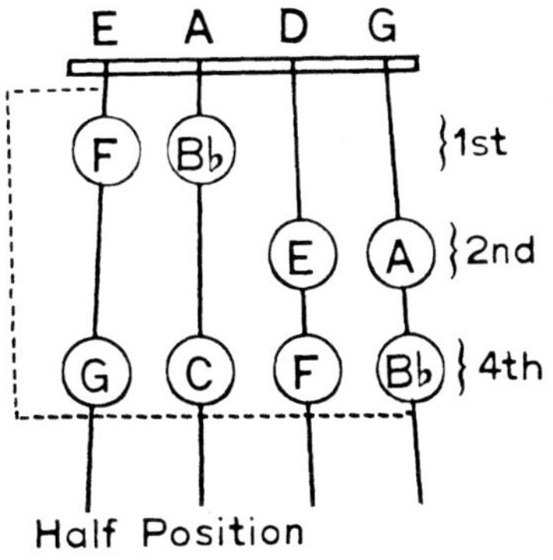

Key of F Major

Détaché Scale

65 

Use whole bow with détaché bowing.

Slurred Scales

Legato (Smooth and connected)

66 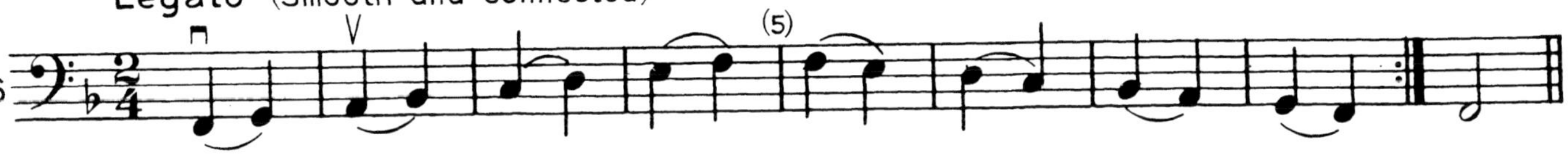

67 

68 

Detached Bowings

Broad and detached

69 

Staccato (Short and detached)

70 

Bow Division

71 

72 

Détaché Scale in Quarter Notes

73 

Use whole bow with détaché bowing.

Broken Chords

74 

75 

Tone Study

76 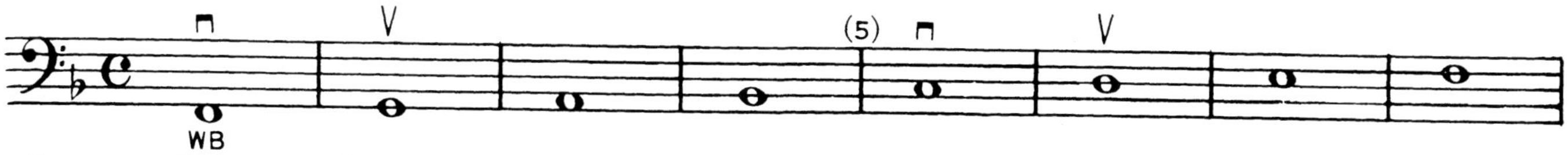

Also practice very slowly, sustaining each tone for EIGHT counts.

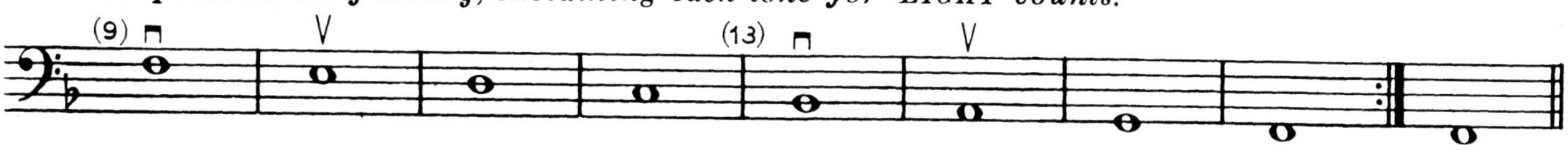

Eighth Notes

77 

Also practice (1) slurring each TWO notes, and (2) slurring each FOUR notes.

Quarter and Eighth Notes

78 

79 

80 

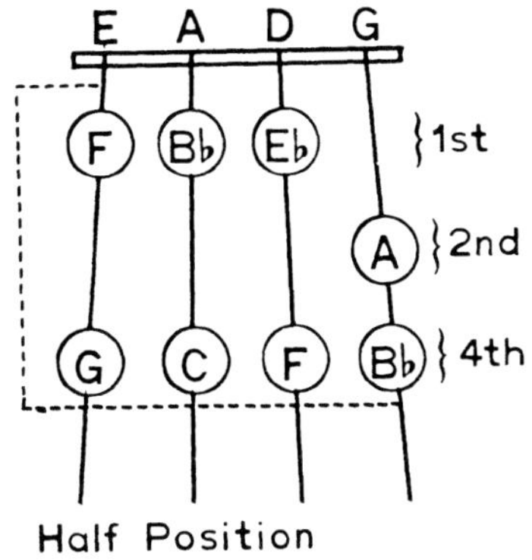

Key of B♭ Major

Détaché Scale

81 

Half Position

Use whole bow with détaché bowing.

Slurred Scales

Legato (Smooth and connected)

82 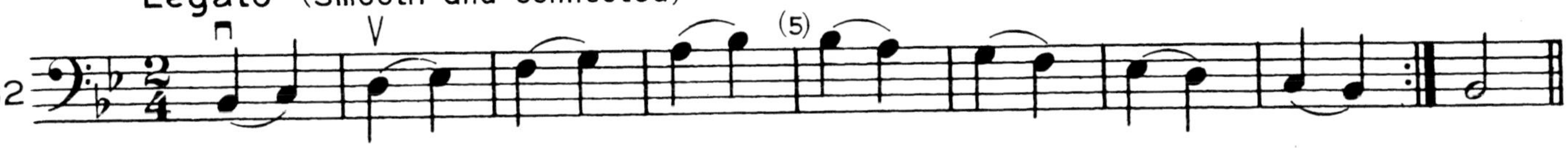

83 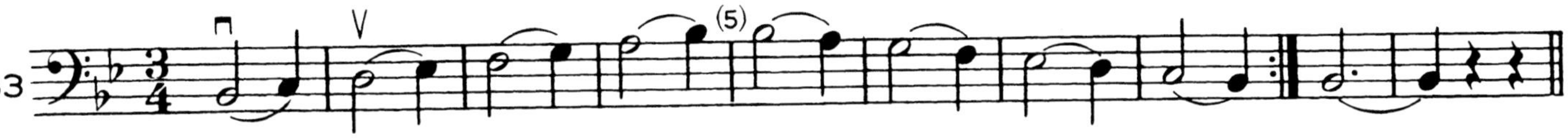

84 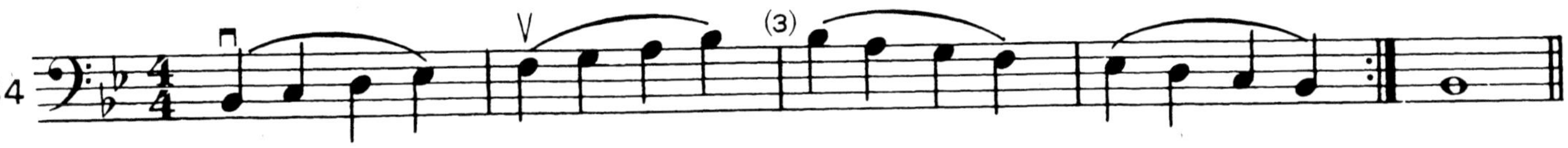

Detached Bowings

Broad and detached

85 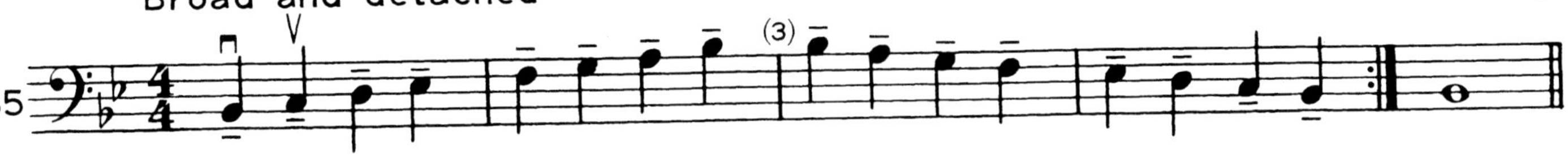

Staccato (Short and detached)

86 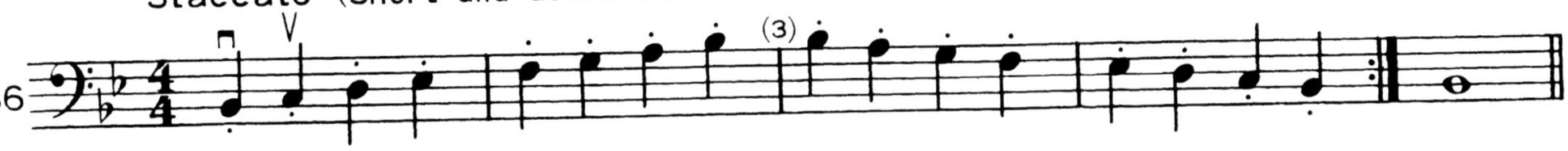

Bow Division

87 

88 

Détaché Scale in Quarter Notes

89 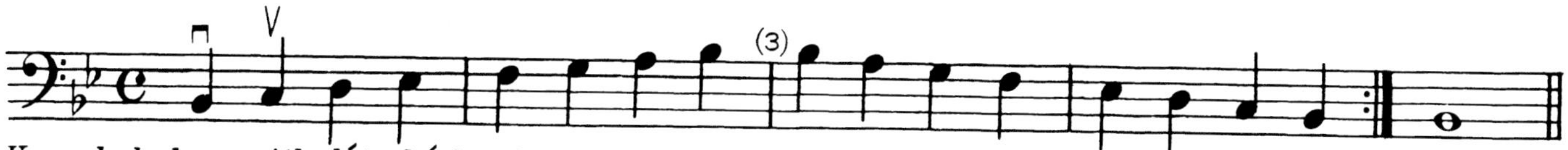

Use whole bow with détaché bowing.

Broken Chords

90 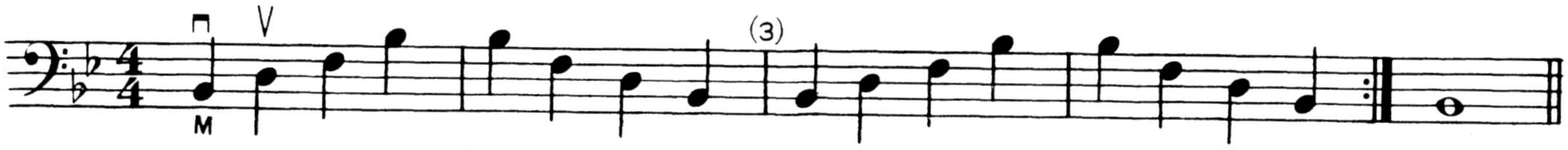

91 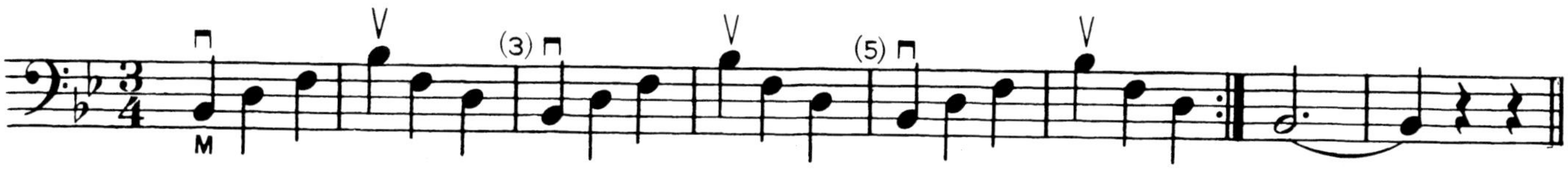

Tone Study

92 

Also practice very slowly, sustaining each tone for EIGHT counts.

Eighth Notes

93 

Also practice (1) slurring each TWO notes, and (2) slurring each FOUR notes.

Quarter and Eighth Notes

94 

95 

96 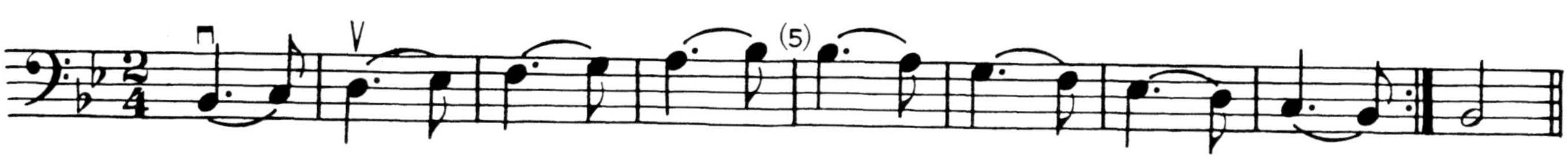

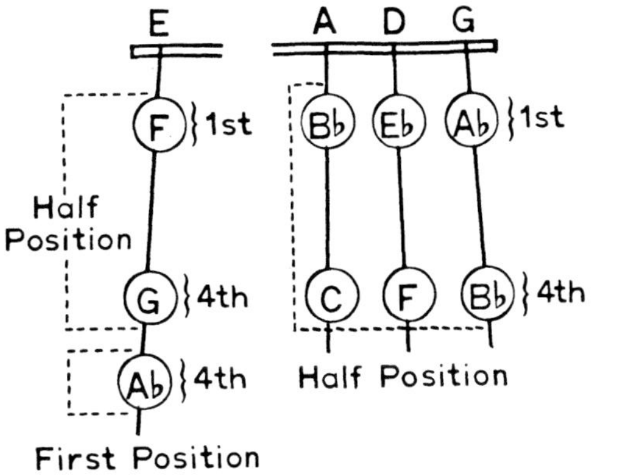

Key of E♭ Major

Détaché Scale

97 

Use whole bow with détaché bowing.

Slurred Scales

Legato (Smooth and connected)

98 

99 

100 

Detached Bowings

Broad and detached

101 

Staccato (Short and detached)

102 

Bow Division

103 

104 

Détaché Scale in Quarter Notes

105 

Use whole bow with détaché bowing.

Broken Chords

106 

107 

Tone Study

108 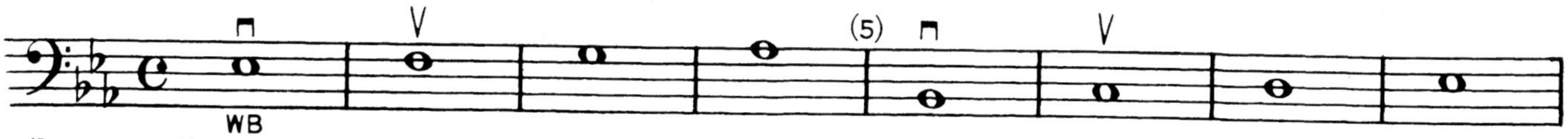

Also practice very slowly, sustaining each tone for EIGHT counts.

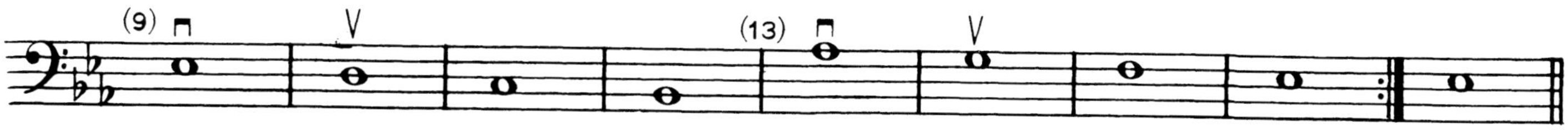

Eighth Notes

109 

Also practice (1) slurring each TWO notes, and (2) slurring each FOUR notes.

Quarter and Eighth Notes

110 

111 

112 

Chromatic Scales

FIRST POSITION FINGERING

Ascending from open string: 0-1-1-2-4 (1 or (2))
Descending from fourth finger: 4-2-1-1-0 (1 or (2))

Where scales ascend or descend directly without a sudden jump in the register, also practice (1) slurring each TWO notes, and (2) slurring each FOUR notes.

113

114
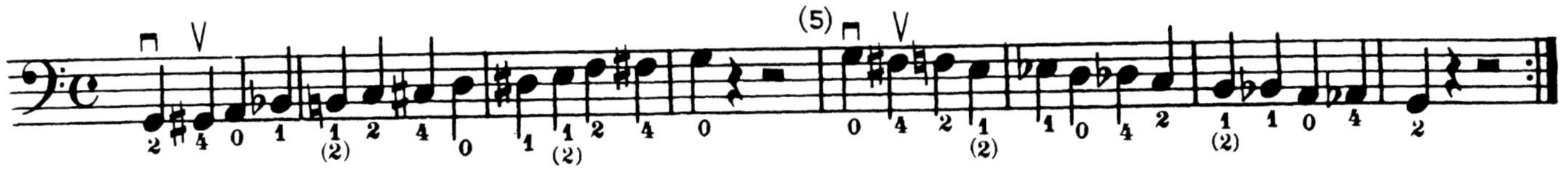

115
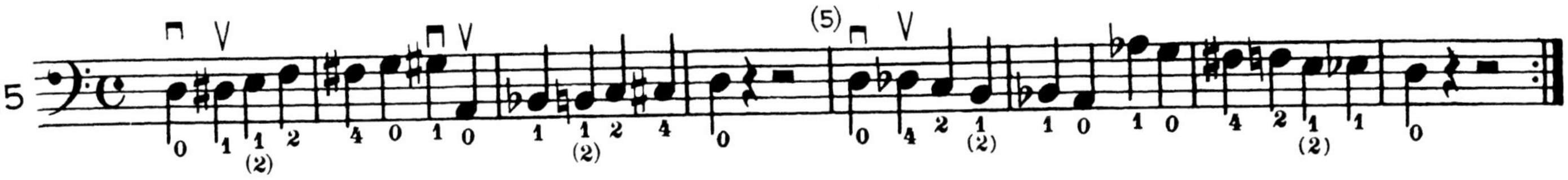

116

117

118
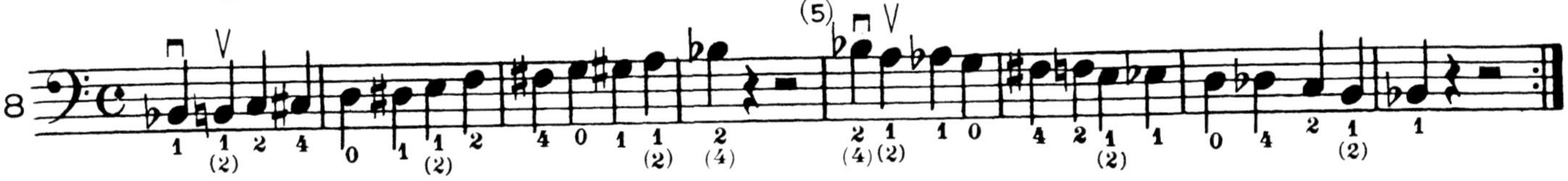

119

Extended Chromatic Scale

Where scale ascends and descends without the jumps in register, also practice (1) slurring each TWO notes, and (2) slurring each FOUR notes.

120
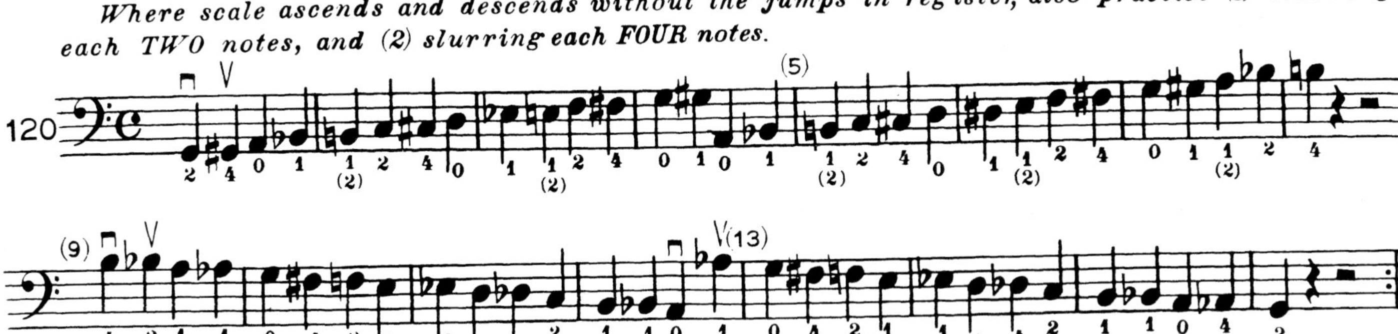